Contents

Skills development in higher education

Short report

CVCP
The voice of
UK universities

DfEE

H.E.Q.E.
HIGHER EDUCATION:
Quality & Employability

Introduction

1.   Skills development is increasingly recognised as being important in making a contribution to the careers of graduates and improving the competitiveness and prosperity of the UK economy. A number of factors, detailed below, are currently acting to promote skills development higher up most higher education institutions' (HEIs) agendas. HEIs, of course, have a key contribution to make to this debate.

2.   Coopers & Lybrand were commissioned in February 1997 to identify strategies which will encourage HEIs:

- to prepare students better for the world of work;

- to place greater emphasis on developing in students the full range of skills - which we have called employability skills - which graduates might bring to their different employment.

3.   The strategies we identify are based on analysing the evidence available from programmes in recent years and from fieldwork with a range of universities and colleges. The Coopers & Lybrand work provided the main input to the final joint CVCP/DfEE report, copies of which are obtainable from CVCP or DfEE.

4.   The purpose of this short report is to summarise some of the key options open to HEIs for the promotion of skills. We begin, however, with a brief outline of the arguments for skill acquisition as presented to us during our fieldwork.

A first definition of employability skills

5.   The Dearing report into higher education (HE) recognised that the needs of employers are complex and not easily defined. Our fieldwork has noted, however, an emerging consensus that the skills concerned in promoting employability should include the following:

- **traditional intellectual skills**: critical evaluation of evidence; the abilities to argue logically, apply theory to practice; to model problems qualitatively and quantitatively; to challenge taken-for-granted assumptions;

- **the 'new' core or key skills**: communication, application of number, information and communications technology, improving one's own performance, working with others;

- **personal attributes**: self-reliance, adaptability, flexibility, *nous*, creativity;

- **knowledge about how organisations work.**

6.   It is important to stress that employability skills include all of these four elements, not just the first three key skills as some have suggested.

The arguments for skill acquisition

7.   There are two main arguments for acquiring or improving employability skills, and

it is important to distinguish between them. They are that:

- developing graduates' skills will improve the performance of people in the labour market, which will in turn improve the UK's competitiveness;

- making graduates more attractive to employers will meet (some of) the criticisms which employers currently make of HEIs and their graduates.

We consider each in turn.

The contribution of skills training to competitiveness

8.   It is becoming generally believed that improved skills training for the UK workforce would lead (or, for some, is leading) to improved competitiveness. It is clear, however, that there are real difficulties in assembling the direct evidence and more research is needed to prove the proposition conclusively. Support for the proposition is provided by comparing the economic contribution graduates make to their own and their employers' prosperity with the contribution made by non-graduates.

9.   It is accepted that in the UK there is a positive economic rate of return on investment in higher education: DfEE estimates that the public rate of return on state investment in HE is around 7 - 9%, and also estimates that the private rate of return to graduates themselves (i.e. through higher salaries) varies between 11 and 17%.

10.   The nature of graduate employment is itself complex and changing. For graduates as for non-graduates, the prospect of a "job for life" is declining: it has been said that some employers appear to want totally committed, totally flexible and totally disposable employees. As a consequence of this trend, however, employers are under pressure to offer employees the opportunity to develop and extend their skills so that they remain sufficiently marketable to survive (and even prosper through) job changes - voluntary or involuntary.

11.   Moreover, an increasing number of graduates are now finding employment with small and medium enterprises (SMEs), who have traditionally little experience in providing the kind of human resource development which has been routine among the larger graduate employers. Not only may graduates joining an SME be expected to "hit the ground running", they may also be expected to take responsibility from day one for their own development.

12.   There has been some research at the individual level on how particular kinds of HE experience impact on the contribution that individual graduates make in their first and subsequent employment. One emerging outcome is that the transfer of skills from one context to another appears to be a learning process which takes time to occur, but which can be supported *inter alia* by appropriately timed short training courses; at the same time, the acquisition of contextual and procedural understanding has to take place in the new context.

Making graduates more attractive to employers

13.   It seems intuitively likely that - other factors being equal - employers would prefer graduates who have received employability skills training over those who have not. But the pattern of such training is so unevenly distributed within and between institutions, and employer perceptions of students are affected by such a range of factors, that it is in fact difficult to find any confirmation of this.

14.   What is interesting is that employers' actual behaviour is not always easy to reconcile with their national lobbying; nor is it necessarily consistent. For instance, employers appear to rate "work experience" very highly when appointing graduates, yet many HEIs report an ongoing shortage of placement opportunities. Moreover employers, as already noted, want early effectiveness from their graduate employees, yet are reluctant to invest in formal or informal induction procedures.

Why (and how) institutions should promote employability skills

15.   The two arguments for promoting the employability skills agenda, taken together, can be argued to have the force of plausibility, despite the absence of conclusive proof. Institutions which do not adopt the skills agenda may therefore increasingly be seen as seriously remiss, and may find it difficult to attract students as a result.

16.   But in promoting the skills agenda, institutions will want to bear in mind some of the hurdles that the early research findings suggest will need to be overcome, namely:

- that the transfer of employability skills from HEI to employer is not a discrete event, nor is it "automatic". It is a learning process in itself;

- that many students appear to remain committed to choosing their programmes on the basis of intrinsic interest rather than presumed relevance to an as yet unknown future job. There is as yet no firm evidence that knowing employability skills are on offer changes an undergraduate's choice of institution, programme or module;

- that students' needs are unlikely to be homogeneous, and in particular that a heavy handed policy of introducing "work skills" into all programmes in an HEI will do little for the increasing proportion of mature students who, even if not currently employed, have considerable experience of the world of work;

- that any major change to HEI curricula and their delivery is likely to have significant cost implications.

Choices and options within HE

17.   To ensure that the employability skills agenda is being adequately delivered within their institution, there are three issues which HEIs will want to address.

The choice between stand alone and embedded approaches

18.   The first issue concerns whether to provide entirely separate "stand alone" modules addressing some or all of the employability skills, or whether to require lecturers to "embed" these skills seamlessly within their teaching and within the learning experiences which they design for students.

19.   The advantages claimed for "embedding" are that they:

- give employability skills the same status as subject knowledge;

- identify the importance of these skills to academic success;

- oblige all lecturers to develop a subject context for employability skills in what they teach.

20.   This contrasts with the stand-alone approach, which may give the skills lower "bolt-on" status and can encourage students not to take them seriously.

21.   In contrast, advocates of the stand-alone approach suggest that:

- discrete employability skills modules ensure that the skills do get covered, by lecturers or instructors competent to teach them;

- modules can be introduced at relatively low cost, without needing to re-equip all facilities or redesign all curricula;

- students can be offered a range of modules targeted at their individual skill needs as perceived or diagnosed;

- in contrast to a generalised commitment to "embedding", which may not change all lecturers' activity, students' entitlement to employability skills is demonstrably in place.

22.   Institutions will need to resolve this debate in a way which makes most sense for them. In the long run, embedding may be more satisfactory, both philosophically and practically; in the shorter term, a high quality stand alone programme may be quicker or easier to introduce, especially if resources are tight.

Acquiring employability skills outside the institution

23.   Incorporating employability skills within campus-based undergraduate programmes is only one way forward, however; institutions will be equally concerned that students have opportunities to gain these skills outside the institution.

24.   Thus HEIs will want to continue to use traditional "work placements" where available and appropriate. They may also want to consider shorter placements or "live projects" as alternatives; these may be more suitable to their programmes, their students, or simply the employment base of their area. In addition, the new "job shops" being found in many HEIs provide opportunities to structure students' term time working experiences in a way which

provides evidence of some employability skills for the student CV.

Employability skills after graduation

25.   The third opportunity for HEIs to make an impact on students' employability skills comes shortly after graduation, and is directed at those students who have so far failed to find employment.

26.   There is a *prima facie* argument that such students' failure may be as a result of apparently weak employability skills - or at least a failure to demonstrate them to employers. For such students, there is increasing pragmatic evidence of the value of intensive, carefully structured programmes which combine training in employability skills, (further) placement experience, and orientation to "the world of work". TECs and SMEs may be able to contribute to the design or delivery of these programmes, and leverage regional and/or EU funding for them; in the long run, however, there is much to be said for funding these programmes through the funding councils' mainstream methodologies.

The HEI context for skills development

27.   We have now argued the case for increased emphasis on employability skills in most institutions. We now need to look at the factors (external and internal) which will promote this emphasis, and those less helpful factors that will need to be managed by

institutions. This will help institutions gauge the success that various approaches to employability skill development are likely to have.

28.   There are clearly a number of external factors promoting the skills agenda at present. These include:

- pressure from the Government, which is concerned to justify its expansion plans for HE and mitigate any perceived decline in the economic rate of return in HE investment;

- the value to an HEI of demonstrating good rates of employment for its graduates - particularly in boosting recruitment;

- the higher priority that the Quality Assurance Agency (QAA) is likely to give to employability skills as it discharges elements of the Dearing agenda;

- the increasing use of externally set and moderated 'core skills tests' at 19+, which will identify skills gaps for HEIs to close;

- the development of records of achievement into the new Progress File, which is expected to pay particular attention to employability skills;

- the increasing importance institutions are giving to meeting continuing professional development needs of graduates, which have synergies with undergraduate employability skill training;

- the increasing importance many HEIs are placing on good links with the employer community in their region;

- the increasing influence which institutional careers services are seeking in the design of the undergraduate curriculum.

29.   In addition, the proposed Institute for Learning and Teaching (ILT) is likely to have employability skills relatively high among its priorities also.

30.   There are however a number of less helpful factors which institutions committed to promoting employability skills development will have to be prepared to overcome. HEIs need to ensure that the strategies adopted to promote the skills agenda take full enough account of these potential difficulties so as not to be quickly thwarted by them. The external factors include:

- the lack of focus on employability skills in the current QA methodology for assessing the quality of teaching (notwithstanding the comment above);

- the dominance of the research agenda in many HEIs;

- the increasing proportion of mature students, which as already noted could be seen as reducing the scale of the problem;

- the influence that professional bodies still exert over curricula; without professional bodies' adoption of the employability skills agenda the freedom of action HEIs have within the programmes that the professional bodies control must be limited;

- the danger of conflicting messages from different players in the local employment network: TECs, Government (regional) Offices, Chambers of Commerce,

development agencies, local authorities are all involved;

- difficulties over making best use of the multiplicity of short term projects which different national public bodies have commissioned to address students' employability skill needs.

31.   There are also a number of potential internal factors which might inhibit employability skills development, and of which senior management in HEIs ought to be aware. These include:

- the diffuse nature of power and accountability in the majority of HEIs: it is not straightforward to ensure that a centrally promulgated agenda (for employability skills or for anything else) is actually implemented in a consistent fashion in all corners of the institution it is intended to reach;

- the lack of training in the management of change within many HEIs;

- the presence of reward and promotions systems which do not always recognise excellence in teaching, let alone excellence in delivering cross-curricular themes like employability skills;

- the lack of sufficient resources to fund the costs of change (both short- and long term).

Strategies for the promotion of the skills agenda

32. The strategies for the promotion of the skills agenda which we suggest here are not mutually exclusive. All represent activities in which many HEIs are already engaged and where there may already be new roles and structures in place. Some HEIs, and departments within HEIs, may want to implement these strategies in different ways (or may find some of the strategies inappropriate to their particular circumstances). The major factors raising the probability of success are summarised below.

Senior management commitment

33. The evidence from successful programmes is that employability skills development is an issue which needs the active support of the Vice-Chancellor/Principal to set the overall tone and signal the importance attached to it. Vice-Chancellors/Principals have a key role to play in endorsing, promoting and supporting the employability skills agenda.

Strategic direction in HEIs

34. Vice-Chancellors/Principals should also consider how ownership of the employability skills agenda is to be achieved by senior management and academic staff at departmental and programme level (ie. amongst those who have lead responsibility for curriculum content, mode of delivery and types of assessment).

35. A useful starting point in this would be for HEIs to undertake an audit of current institutional structures to assess the extent to which they are receptive to the employability skills agenda. For example, institutional structures may, at present, be geared towards the requirements of the research assessment exercise, funding council statutory returns, and teaching quality assessments. Changes need not involve radical restructuring but rather might consider how existing structures can be adapted to the needs of the employability skills agenda. Employability skills development will require a different focus, for example a more proactive approach towards employers and regional economic development agencies and the systematic collection and analysis of labour market information.

36. Mechanisms which others have found helpful include:

- the inclusion of (meaningful) references to employability skills within mission statements and institutional, faculty and departmental academic plans;

- appointing "skills co-ordinators" and establishing support networks, which can provide a crucial link between the strategic direction of the institution and its operational implementation;

- providing financial injections to kick start new developments and changing institutional reward and promotions systems to give greater recognition to excellence in teaching and curriculum development, including their employability skills dimensions.

Implementation strategies in HEIs

37.   HEIs should assess which skills they will focus on and how they intend to establish skills development - via stand alone modules or via embedding skills development within the curriculum (or by a combination of both these approaches).   As already noted, our fieldwork for this study has shown that stand alone employability skills programmes can be effective in improving the recognition and acceptance of skills training. On the other hand, the fieldwork also shows that some of the most successful and lasting skills programmes are those where the training is embedded within the academic subject curriculum.

Quality assurance processes

38.   An effective lever for change within HEIs will be for internal quality assurance processes to be explicitly linked to the teaching of employability skills. This approach is consistent with the recommendations in the HE Dearing report for programme specifications to be developed which set out the desired outcomes of programmes, including knowledge and skills.

Assessment

39.   HEIs' internal programme approval and validation processes should include checks that employability skills are not only acquired and practised but also that they are assessed appropriately. HEIs should consider the level of resource and effort that they are prepared to

commit to the assessment of employability skills, and identify the point(s) in a student's academic career at which this assessment will occur.

Monitoring and evaluation

40.   HEIs should ensure that the internal monitoring and evaluation of employability skills training is built into their programme review processes. HEIs should consider the level of resources that they are prepared to commit to external monitoring and evaluation, such as the systematic sampling of graduates and their employment patterns following completion of their degree programmes. The learning from such exercises can be very helpful in refining institutions' skills development approaches.

Student input and feedback

41.   Students as consumers of HE can influence HEIs through the outputs they demand from academic degree programmes and through the role they play on institutional decision making committees. HEIs should ensure that, in developing their institutional strategy to promote employability skills development, they consult and involve their students (and student unions). It will be important for HEIs to recognise the full range of student experience, including mature and part-time students who may already possess strong employability skills.

Staff training, development and support

42.　HEIs should consider mechanisms to promote the development of employability skills training at institutional level and ensure that their staff are at the forefront in developing this agenda. A number of the successful mechanisms that we have observed are detailed in the full report. They include:

- incorporating the development and assessment of employability skills as a core part of the initial training which all lecturers receive;

- setting up an institutional Learning and Assessment Centre, staffed by appropriately qualified staff, to advise on curriculum design and assess employability skills;

- reviewing institutional reward and promotion procedures to consider the mechanisms which could be adopted to recognise excellence in teaching and curriculum development.

43.　HEIs collectively have already been consulted on the criteria that should be required for the accreditation of teachers in higher education. At least one aspect of these criteria should be related to teaching employability skills. The Institute for Learning and Teaching could also provide a focus for research, development and training in all aspects of the teaching of employability skills.

The role of careers services

44.　Institutional careers services play an essential role as facilitators in the operation of the graduate labour market, since they interact both with employers on the demand side and graduates on the supply side. There is thus considerable scope to develop and refine their role.

45.　HEIs should consider the extent to which their careers services can play a more active role within their institutions, and the resources that might be committed to supporting this more active role. Vice-Chancellors/Principals in particular could be influential in endorsing a higher profile for careers services within the curriculum. Again, the full report sets out those areas where careers services might play a useful role: from closer involvement in programme accreditation, evaluation and review, to providing a service to alumni.

Employers and employer organisations

46.　Employers and employer-led organisations, as consumers of graduates, should be important influences on the context and content of employability skills training programmes. As recommended by Dearing, HEIs should review the extent and nature of their existing links with employers and employer organisations so as both to improve the interface and to enhance the responsiveness of their institutions to employer needs. The review will need to consider how the institution will interact externally with employers, employer organisations and other agencies; it will also need to look at the extent to which partnerships with employers can be enhanced and developed.

Regional Development Agencies

47.   The importance of the regional dimension to HEI development has been signalled as a concern of the new government, and is endorsed by the HE Dearing report. We recommend that HEIs should consider whether there are advantages in a single agency taking on a key role in co-ordinating HEI-related activities on behalf of the TECs, Chambers and other regional employer-led bodies and becoming the primary agency responsible for representing the regional economic agenda and interests to HEIs.

Other stakeholders

48.   We believe that there are a number of actions which should also be taken at the national level by other key stakeholders to enable and assist HEIs to take employability skills training more seriously.

49.   The key stakeholders include those below; we briefly indicate the actions which we believe they should take:

- the Funding Councils and QAA - by virtue of the role they play in influencing programme development and quality assurance and control. These organisations should ensure that HEIs demonstrate the place of employability skills as a central part of undergraduates' academic programmes;

- NUS / Student Unions - because of the role they play in influencing students and HEIs. They should use their influence within institutions to ensure that the employability skills agenda is treated with the importance it deserves;

- Regional Development Agencies - because they are likely to emerge as key influencers of the economic and educational context within which employability skills development will occur. RDAs could take the lead in co-ordinating the currently somewhat fragmented messages which HEIs receive from regional bodies and groups, and help resolve the plethora of initiatives to which many HEIs are required to respond in this area;

- Employers and employer organisations - as "consumers" of employability skills. Employer organisations could encourage their members to provide increased opportunities for work placement and experience, and to take the induction of their new graduates more seriously;

- Teachers' Unions - because of the role they play in influencing teachers and HEIs. The unions represent a potentially powerful source of pressure on the new ILT to ensure that employability skills training is central to its thinking;

- Association of Graduate Careers Advisory Services (AgCAS) - as influencers of the careers services which have close working relationships with both students and employers. There is likely to be considerable scope for AgCAS, at a national level, to promote the case for a more active role for careers services within HEIs - for example in the curriculum field.

50.   It would also be useful if the actions of the key stakeholders as proposed here were co-ordinated, to ensure the consistency and maximum impact of their messages. This co-ordination role could be undertaken by any one of a number of agencies involved in the field.

Conclusion

51.   The recommendations for change set out here provide a sound basis for implementing effective approaches to skills development; they represent a challenging, but we believe achievable, agenda. All HEIs should, we believe, now move speedily first to define then to implement their own change agendas.

Appendix A

Membership of the Project Steering Group

Professor Leslie Wagner, Vice-Chancellor, Leeds Metropolitan University (Chair)
Professor Ken Gregory, Warden, Goldsmiths' College, University of London
James Wright, Vice-Chancellor, University of Newcastle
Professor Gary Crossley, Deputy Director, Surrey Institute of Art & Design
Dr Peter Wright, Assistant Director, Higher Education Quality Council (now the Quality Assurance Agency)
Richard Brown, Chief Executive, Council for Industry and Higher Education
Cliff Allan, Head of Teaching and Learning Policy, Higher Education Funding Council for England
Steve Ingham, Head of Operations Team, Department for Education and Employment
Keith McMaster, Development Manager, Department for Education and Employment
Sue Otter, DfEE consultant
Patricia Ambrose, Policy Adviser, CVCP

Coopers & Lybrand Project Team

Quentin Thompson, Partner
John Atkins, Lead Consultant
Chris Snell, Project Manager
Pearl Roberts, Project Officer
Professor Madeleine Atkins, Dean of the Faculty of Education, University of Newcastle